MENTAL HEALTH AND WELLNESS

BY BRIGHTNEST PRESS

A Guide to Navigating Life's Challenges with Balance and Positivity

CONTENTS

1. INTRODUCTION TO MENTAL HEALTH AND WELLNESS

Importance of mental health, how it's just as vital as physical health, and the purpose of this book

2. UNDERSTANDING MENTAL HEALTH

Mental health is more than the absence of mental illness; it's a state of balance in our thoughts, feelings, and behaviors

3. RECOGNIZING COMMON MENTAL HEALTH ISSUES

Recognizing the symptoms is the first step to addressing them. Knowing you're not alone can make all the difference.

4. THE IMPORTANCE OF SELF-CARE

Self-care is not selfish; it's essential. When you take care of yourself, you're better equipped to take care of others.

5. BUILDING RESILIENCE

Resilience doesn't mean avoiding stress but learning to navigate it gracefully.

6. MANAGING STRESS

Stress is a part of life, but it doesn't have to control you. Simple habits can help you stay centered even on challenging days.

7. CULTIVATING POSITIVE RELATIONSHIPS

Positive relationships provide emotional support, reduce feelings of loneliness, and contribute to a sense of belonging.

8. MINDFULNESS AND MEDITATION

Gratitude and mindfulness are powerful tools for cultivating a positive mindset and reducing stress.

9. THE ROLE OF PHYSICAL HEALTH IN MENTAL WELLNESS

Your body and mind are closely connected; caring for one helps the other.

10. SETTING PERSONAL GOALS FOR MENTAL WELLNESS

Setting personal goals helps you stay motivated and gives you a sense of direction.

Hello, and thank you for joining me on this journey toward mental wellness! My name is Shelly, and I have been passionate about mental health and well-being for as long as I can remember. My own journey began with a desire to better understand the complexities of mental health, a field that deeply affects us all yet is often overlooked. Over the years, through both personal experiences and professional work, I have dedicated myself to learn about effective strategies for managing stress, fostering resilience, and maintaining mental and emotional balance. I am thrilled to share insights, practices, and actionable steps with you through this eBook. My goal is to provide you with clear, approachable guidance that you can integrate into your life to nurture your own wellness.

Shelly Solinus

INTRODUCTION TO MENTAL HEALTH AND WELLNESS

Mental health is the foundation of a balanced life. It influences how we think, feel, and behave as we manage the ups and downs of life. Just like physical health, it requires care and attention. This book offers a guide to mental wellness, showing that it's not about reaching perfection but about finding balance. Embrace this journey to a healthier, more resilient you.

UNDERSTANDING MENTAL HEALTH

Mental health refers to our emotional, psychological, and social well-being. It affects how we think, make decisions, and relate to others. Mental health exists on a spectrum from thriving to struggling and it's perfectly normal to fluctuate. Mental wellness is a process, and understanding this can help remove stigma. Remember, seeking balance is key, not seeking flawlessness.

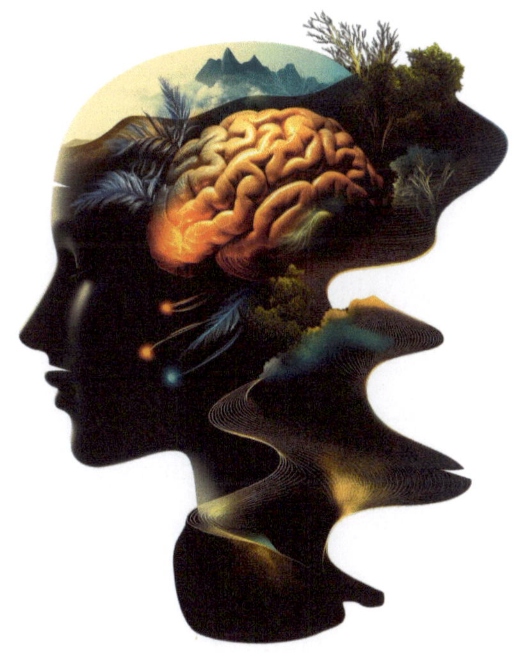

RECOGNIZING COMMON MENTAL HEALTH ISSUES

Recognizing common mental health issues is a crucial part of maintaining wellness, as it helps you identify when something feels off and know when to seek support. This chapter focuses on some of the most prevalent mental health challenges people face, such as anxiety, depression, stress, and burnout. Each of these conditions can impact a person's daily life, relationships, and overall well-being, and understanding them can help reduce stigma and promote early intervention.

Anxiety often shows up as excessive worry, restlessness, or feeling "on edge." Recognizing these symptoms can be the first step toward addressing anxiety and finding coping techniques, like deep breathing or mindfulness, that help calm the mind. Depression, on the other hand, can involve prolonged sadness, a loss of interest in activities you once enjoyed, fatigue, and difficulty concentrating. Understanding that these symptoms are more than just "feeling down" can help you or someone you know seek appropriate support.

Stress and burnout are also common challenges, particularly in fast-paced work or personal environments. Stress often results from feeling overwhelmed by demands, while burnout tends to develop over time when stress is prolonged and unaddressed, leaving a person feeling physically and emotionally drained. Recognizing the early signs of burnout—such as constant exhaustion, decreased performance, and withdrawal from social activities—can help you take preventive actions to protect your mental well-being.

By understanding these common mental health issues, you're better equipped to recognize when you or someone else may need support, allowing you to take action sooner rather than later. This chapter provides an overview of these conditions, emphasizing that experiencing any of them doesn't mean there's something "wrong" with you. Rather, it's a normal part of the human experience, and there are effective ways to manage and seek support for mental health.

THE IMPORTANCE OF SELF-CARE

Self-care is essential for maintaining mental health and overall well-being. In our fast-paced lives, it's easy to prioritize work, family, and other responsibilities over our personal needs, often resulting in stress, burnout, and a decline in mental health. But taking time to care for oneself is not selfish—it's necessary for sustaining energy, motivation, and resilience.

Why Self-Care Matters

Self-care is an act of acknowledging
your own needs. When we dedicate
time to rejuvenate, we can handle
challenges more effectively and enjoy
 life's moments with greater presence.

The benefits of self-care extend beyond mental wellness, positively
influencing physical health, productivity, and our relationships. By
making self-care a regular practice, we can prevent the build-up of
stress and make healthier choices in every aspect of life.

Types of Self-Care

Self-care comes in many forms, including physical, emotional, and social self-care:

Physical Self-Care:
Activities like exercise, sleep, balanced nutrition, and relaxing practices (like stretching or gentle yoga) help maintain energy and physical resilience. Our bodies and minds are closely connected, so physical care can reduce stress and elevate our moods.

Emotional Self-Care:

Practicing self-compassion, allowing yourself to experience a range of emotions, journaling, or talking with a trusted friend or counselor can help you process and release difficult emotions. Emotional self-care helps build a positive relationship with oneself, boosting self-worth.

Social Self-Care:

Maintaining strong social connections with friends, family, and colleagues nurtures your sense of belonging. Meaningful relationships provide comfort and perspective, offering support and joy.

Incorporating Self-Care into Daily Life

Self-care doesn't need to be time-consuming. It can be as simple as setting aside 10 minutes each day to reflect, meditate, or do something you enjoy. Here are a few ways to include self-care in your daily life.

Set Boundaries:
Protect your time and energy by learning to say no to unnecessary commitments that add stress or drain you.

Create a Routine:
Build small self-care practices into your daily routine, such as a few minutes of morning breathing exercises, an evening walk, or a quick check-in with yourself.

Prioritize Sleep and Rest:
Quality rest is foundational for mental wellness. Aim for 7-9 hours of sleep per night, and try to wind down at least an hour before bed.

Practice Mindfulness:
Use mindfulness exercises to stay connected to the present moment, which reduces stress and improves emotional resilience.

The Long–Term Benefits of Self-Care

Consistent self-care can help prevent mental health issues, improve self-awareness, and promote overall happiness and satisfaction. By putting your well-being first, you're equipping yourself with the strength and balance to face life's demands with greater calm, clarity, and focus.

BUILDING RESILIENCE

Resilience is our ability to bounce back from setbacks. It doesn't mean avoiding difficulties but learning to handle them. Resilience grows through small actions: setting achievable goals, practicing gratitude, and maintaining a positive outlook. Every time we face a challenge, we build resilience, creating inner strength that helps us cope with life's surprises

MANAGING STRESS

In our busy, often overwhelming lives, stress is a common experience. While a certain level of stress can motivate and keep us alert, chronic stress can harm our mental and physical health. Managing stress effectively is key to maintaining balance, productivity, and overall well-being.

Understanding Stress and Its Impact

Stress is the body's response to any demand or challenge, often referred to as the "fight-or-flight" response. While this reaction can be helpful in urgent situations, prolonged exposure to stress triggers can lead to burnout, exhaustion, and various health problems, such as anxiety, high blood pressure, and sleep issues. Recognizing when stress is taking over is the first step toward managing it.

Practical Strategies for Managing Stress

Effectively managing stress involves learning healthy coping mechanisms and making small changes that can have a big impact over time. Here are some strategies to help reduce and manage stress:

Identify Your Stressors

Start by recognizing the situations, environments, or relationships that cause you stress. Keeping a stress journal can help you pinpoint these sources, allowing you to address them more effectively.

Set Realistic Boundaries

Often, stress arises from taking on too many responsibilities or committing to things that go beyond our capacity. Learning to say no and setting boundaries around your time and energy can reduce stress significantly.

Prioritize Physical Activity

Exercise is a natural stress reliever. Physical activity releases endorphins, which improve mood and reduce stress. Even a short daily walk or stretching routine can make a difference in how you feel.

Stay Connected

Talking with friends, family, or a counselor can provide emotional support and new perspectives on stressful situations. Social connections play a powerful role in helping you feel understood and supported, which reduces feelings of stress and isolation.

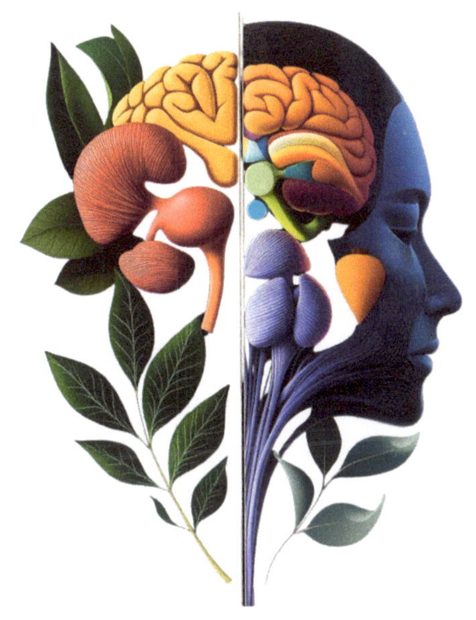

Practice Relaxation Techniques

Techniques such as deep breathing exercises, progressive muscle relaxation, and guided imagery can calm the nervous system and provide relief from stress. Try dedicating a few minutes each day to these practices to build a sense of inner calm.

Adopt Time Management Skills

Learning to prioritize tasks and create a manageable schedule can prevent stress from piling up. Breaking larger tasks into smaller, more achievable steps also reduces the overwhelm that can come from facing big responsibilities all at once.

Developing a Resilient Mindset

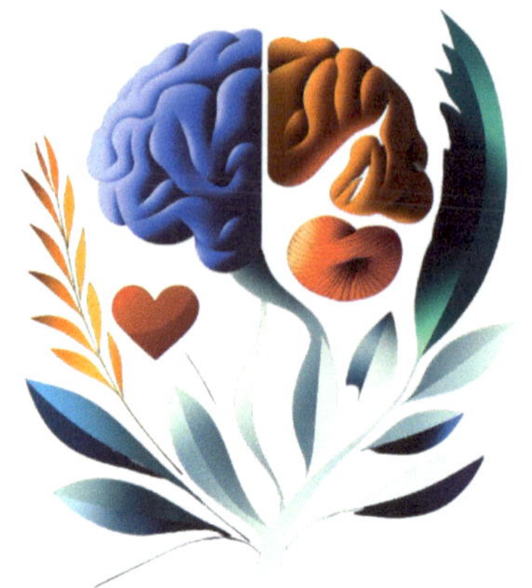

In addition to practical strategies, building resilience is key to handling stress. Resilience involves adapting to challenges with a positive, proactive mindset. By viewing obstacles as learning experiences rather than insurmountable barriers, you can reduce stress's emotional impact. Practicing gratitude, focusing on solutions, and embracing a growth mindset can foster resilience, enabling you to navigate stress more effectively.

Long-Term Benefits of Managing Stress
Managing stress is not just about immediate relief but about creating a healthier lifestyle overall. Effective stress management can improve mood, strengthen relationships, increase productivity, and protect against various health problems. Over time, these practices can help you become more balanced, energized, and capable of enjoying life fully.

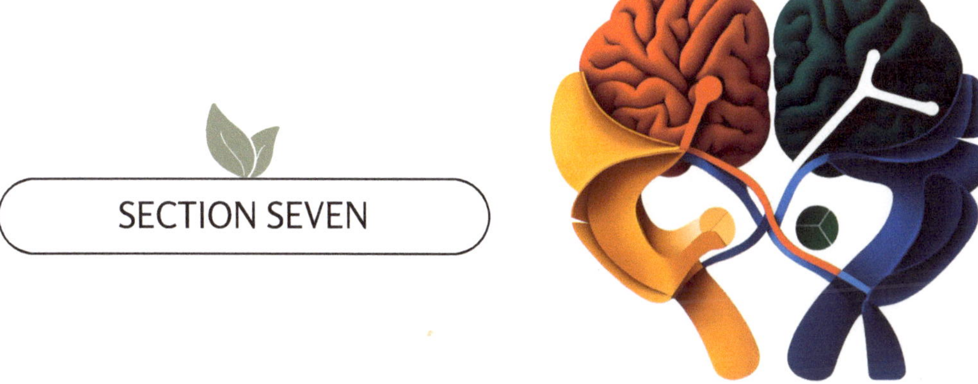

CULTIVATING POSITIVE RELATIONSHIPS

Human connections are essential for mental well-being. Positive relationships provide emotional support, reduce feelings of loneliness, and contribute to a sense of belonging. This chapter discusses the importance of nurturing meaningful connections and practicing healthy communication. It emphasizes setting boundaries, being an active listener, and spending quality time with loved ones. Cultivating positive relationships strengthens your social support network, offering comfort during tough times and enhancing your sense of joy and purpose.

MINDFULNESS AND MEDITATION

Mindfulness is about staying present, fully engaging in each moment without judgment. This practice, often paired with meditation, allows us to observe our thoughts without reacting to them. Start with a few minutes of quiet each day, focusing on your breath. Mindfulness and meditation bring clarity and calm, helping us respond thoughtfully rather than react impulsively.

THE ROLE OF PHYSICAL HEALTH IN MENTAL WELLNESS

What we eat and how active we are play a critical role in mental health. Balanced nutrition fuels the brain, stabilizes mood, and improves focus, while regular physical activity releases endorphins, which reduce stress and promote happiness. This chapter provides guidance on incorporating healthy foods and exercise into your routine, explaining how good nutrition and physical activity can uplift your mind and body. Simple changes in diet and physical activity can lead to lasting improvements in both mental and physical wellness.

SETTING PERSONAL GOALS FOR MENTAL WELLNESS

Setting personal goals helps you stay motivated and gives you a sense of direction. This chapter explores the benefits of creating mental wellness goals—such as improving self-care habits, enhancing relationships, or managing stress better—and how to achieve them using the SMART (Specific, Measurable, Achievable, Relevant, Time-bound) framework. Clear, achievable goals empower you to make steady progress, building self-confidence and a sense of accomplishment. This chapter concludes with tips for setting goals that align with your mental health journey and support your overall well-being.

Be mindful while setting the goals

The first step is to understand what you want to achieve. Ask yourself what areas of your mental well-being need the most attention—maybe it's reducing stress, improving self-confidence, or developing better coping strategies for difficult emotions. Once you've identified your focus areas, break them down into smaller, achievable steps. For example, if your goal is to reduce anxiety, you might start by setting aside five minutes daily for mindfulness or deep breathing exercises.

Another essential aspect of goal-setting is consistency. Mental wellness is a journey that requires regular practice, and setting small, achievable milestones along the way can help you stay motivated. Instead of expecting immediate results, celebrate small victories, like journaling every day for a week or reaching out to friends more often. These small steps can build confidence and reinforce positive habits over time.

Finally, remember that setbacks are a normal part of any journey. Instead of feeling discouraged, use these moments to reassess your goals, make adjustments, and remind yourself why you started. Setting goals for mental wellness is not about perfection but about progress and self-compassion. By setting meaningful, achievable goals, you create a path toward lasting mental wellness that you can sustain and grow with over time.